CW00557321

Tadpole Rag
and
Caterpillar Boogie

by Douglas Wootton
edited by Alison Hedger

Two fun mini-musicals for children aged 3 to 7 years
Factual life-cycles of frogs and butterflies
Each musical has five songs and lasts approximately 15 minutes

TEACHER'S BOOK
Complete with script and music

TADPOLE RAG SONGS
1. Frog Song
2. Something Squidgy
3. Tadpole Rag
4. Quack!
5. Frogs Are Amazing

CATERPILLAR BOOGIE SONGS
1. Butterfly Sparkle
2. Caterpillar Boogie
3. Hip-Hop, Here Come The Birds
4. Caterpillar Lullaby
5. Fly, Butterfly, Fly

© Copyright 1998 Golden Apple Productions
A division of Chester Music Limited
14-15 Berners Street, London W1T 3LJ

Order No. GA11957

ISBN 978-1-84938-336-3

TADPOLE RAG

The first little musical in this book was written for children 3 to 7 years old. It tells clearly in words and song the life cycle of the frog, an important topic at school. TADPOLE RAG can be performed as a costumed mini-musical with lots of fun movements and dance. Alternatively, the songs and narration can be delivered as a concert piece. Each of the songs is fun to sing at any time. The piano score is deliberately simple to make it attractive to school pianists, but should you wish to embellish the music given, please do so. The matching audio CD has a full musical backing.

CAST

Narrator(s)   Either an adult, or divide the script between various children. The narration must be delivered slowly and clearly with children using their biggest voices.

Frogs
School Children
Teacher   With frog spawn and a big glass bowl
Tadpoles
Ducks

No stage directions are given, so allowing teachers to act out, or not, according to what is needed. All the children learn all the songs, with actions and dances from the character parts as befits the story and lyrics.

To make frog spawn, use clear bubble pack with black dots marked out on each bubble with a black felt tip pen.

WHAT IS A RAG?

Rag is short for Ragtime, a late nineteenth century term given to a distinctive style of music of Afro-American origin. The regularly accented beat in the bass provides a firm foundation for an energetic syncopation above. The earliest composers were from St Louis. Tom Turpin's 1895 Harlem Rag and Scott Joplin's Maple Leaf Rag established a popular style that was enjoyed all over America by the turn of the twentieth century. The Rag conquered Europe with the publication of Irving Berlin's Alexander's Rag Time Band in 1911. Ragtime became Jazz, a term first used in Chicago about 1916, and applied to orchestral Ragtime. Pure piano Ragtime continued to exist independently with its infectious energy and fun.

Narration
If you stand by a pond,
Where it's damp all round,
And listen very carefully
You may hear this sound.

All Children
Rivet, rivet, rivet. Rivet, rivet, rivet.
(*imitating croaking frogs*)

Narration
Or in a meadow,
By a stream
Where the water's clear.
If you're very lucky,
Then you might hear . . .

All Children
Rivet, rivet, rivet. Rivet, rivet, rivet.
(*imitating croaking frogs*)

SONG ONE   # FROG SONG

(*croaking*)
**Rivet, rivet, rivet.
Rivet, rivet, rivet.**

1. **Frogs, frogs, frogs, frogs, singing tonight.
    Sing for their lady frogs till it's daylight.
    And all of the rivers, the lakes and the bogs
    Ring to the singing of hundreds of frogs.**
(*croaking*)
    **Rivet, rivet, rivet.
    Rivet, rivet, rivet.**

2. **Frogs like to sing when the weather is wet,
    'Round about evening and when the sun sets.
    And all of the rivers, the lakes and the bogs
    Ring to the singing of hundreds and,
    Hundreds and, hundreds and,
    Hundreds and, hundreds and,
    Hundreds of frogs.**
(*croaking*)
    Rivet!

*Repeat the music for a **Frogs' Prance** – lots of jumping around.*

Narration

"But what is a frog?"
We wanted to know.

"Where do they come from,
Where do they go?"

"How do they live
And how do they grow?"

Then teacher, who is very wise,
Said, "I will bring you something
As a big, big surprise."

SONG TWO

SOMETHING SQUIDGY

One day teacher brought to school
Something squidgy from a pool.
It was strange and wob-bl-y.
Looked like a jelly on a plate to me.
She said "This is called frog spawn,
Tadpoles waiting to be born."
We said "How long will that be?"
She said "You must wait and see."
So we put it in a bowl.
Waited for our first tadpole.

} **twice**

Narration

In the spawn there were little black dots,
And they began to wriggle – lots and lots.

And then one day what did we see?
Lots of little tadpoles had wriggled free.

SONG THREE

TADPOLE RAG

1. Swim little tadpole. We're glad to see
That you are just what a tadpole's supposed to be.
You've got a nice little tail and a big black head.
And you came from the frog spawn, like teacher said.
Swim little tadpole, swim little tadpole,
Swim with your wrig-gl-y tail.

2. Swim little tadpole. Now you're in luck,
'Cause there are no hungry fishes to eat you up.
So you're as safe as can be in your big glass bowl,
Because there's nothing to swallow a small tadpole.
Swim little tadpole, swim little tadpole,
Swim with your wrig-gl-y tail.

Repeat music for **Tadpoles' Dance**

Narration

** (Show a big picture or
model with external gills)*

At first the tadpoles looked like this
With gills to breath in water.

But later on they disappeared
And tiny little legs appeared.

(Show picture)

And so they slowly changed into
Baby frogs complete.
With long back legs and four webbed feet,
We thought it was amazing.

Then teacher said "We'll put them in
A pond where they can live and swim."

But when we got there, oh dear me!
The ducks looked at them hungrily.

* Refer to picture on page 16

5

SONG FOUR	# QUACK!

During the song, ducks waddle around and flap their wings

1. Quack, quack, quack, quack.
   Hurry up and throw them back.
   Baby frogs make a tasty snack.
   Quack, quack, quack, quack.
   Quack, quack, quack, quack, quack, quack, quack.

2. Quack, quack, quack, quack.
   Throw them in and set them free.
   Then we'll gobble them up for tea,
   Quack, quack, quack, quack.
   Quack, quack, quack, quack, quack, quack, quack.

Narration

So teacher who is very fond
Of frogs, said "I will make a pond,
And keep them in my garden.
And they will eat the snails and slugs
And lots of pesky flies and bugs,
And you shall come and see them."
Those little frogs just grew and grew,
Till one day they had tadpoles too!

SONG FIVE	# FROGS ARE AMAZING

1. Frogs are amazing.
   Frogs are amazing.
   They begin life as frog spawn, and
   Then as tadpoles they are born.

2. Frogs are amazing.
   Frogs are amazing.
   As the tadpoles slowly grow,
   Well, they turn into frogs, you know.

3.   **Frogs are amazing.**
        Frogs are amazing.
        They can breath in water and on land,
        'Cause they're amphibian.

4.   **Frogs are amazing.**
        Frogs are amazing.
        They can jump and they can swim.
        A frog is an amazing thing.

Narration   We hope you have enjoyed our show.
                     Just one more thing before we go.

                     A big long word for your big word list –
                     If you want to study frogs you'll be a
                     HERPETOLOGIST!

Everyone   Bye-bye.

Wave and exit to repeat of music to song three **TADPOLE RAG**

THE END

1
FROG SONG

Cue: Rivet, rivet, rivet. Rivet, rivet, rivet.
After singing the song, repeat the music for a Frogs' Prance

9

2
SOMETHING SQUIDGY

Cue: "I will bring you something as a big, big surprise."

Helpful tip: listen to the matching audio CD to catch the rhythm of the introduction

3
TADPOLE RAG (also music for finale)

Cue: Lots of little tadpoles had wriggled free.

With a rhythmic swing ♩ = 120

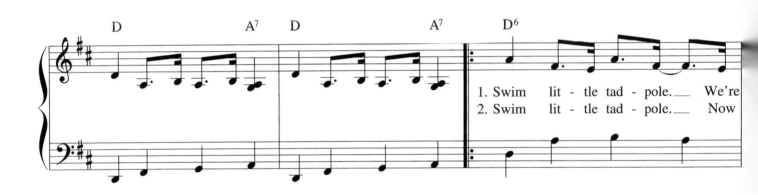

1. Swim lit - tle tad - pole.___ We're
2. Swim lit - tle tad - pole.___ Now

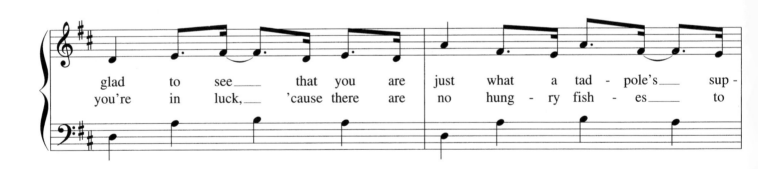

glad to see___ that you are just what a tad - pole's___ sup -
you're in luck,___ 'cause there are no hung - ry fish - es___ to

- posed to be.___ You've got a nice lit - tle tail and___ a
eat you up.___ So you're as safe as can be in___ your

See page 2 for What Is A Rag?

After singing the song, repeat the music for **Tadpoles' Dance**

4
QUACK!

Cue: But when we got there, oh dear me! The ducks looked at them hungrily.

During the song, ducks waddle around and flap their wings.

1. Quack, quack, quack, quack. Hur - ry up and throw them back.
2. Quack, quack, quack, quack. Throw them in and set them free.

Ba - by frogs___ make a tas - ty snack.
Then we'll gob - ble them___ up for tea.

Quack, quack, quack, quack. Quack, quack, quack, quack, quack, quack, quack.

5
FROGS ARE AMAZING

Cue: Those little frogs just grew and grew, till one day they had tadpoles too!

CATERPILLAR BOOGIE

The second little musical was also written for children aged 3 to 7 years. It tells simply and clearly in words and song the life cycle of the butterfly, an important topic at this age. CATERPILLAR BOOGIE can be performed as a concert piece or be a useful classroom resource for individual songs. It was, however, conceived by Douglas Wootton as a theatrical experience. As with TADPOLE RAG there is a lot of scope for creative design, movement and dance as well as, of course, singing. The very simple piano part will be attractive to school pianists. Please embellish the score if you wish and repeat the music for dance and extra singing as required.

CAST

Narrator(s)	Either an adult, or divide the script between various children. The narration must be delivered very slowly and clearly with children using their biggest voices.
Butterflies	
Caterpillars	
Lettuces	
Cabbages	
Birds	
Gardener	With chemical spray

No stage directions are given, so allowing teachers to act out, or not, according to what is needed. All the children sing all the songs with actions and dances from the character parts as befits the story and lyrics.

WHAT IS A BOOGIE?

Boogie is short for Boogie Woogie, a term given to a nineteenth century style of American piano jazzy music. The style probably originated in St Louis but others believe Boogie Woogie began in Kansas City. By the turn of the twentieth century this distinctive style in $\frac{4}{4}$ time was know in Orleans and also went under the name of Honky-tonk, Barrel-house and Eight-to-the-bar. The real stronghold of Boogie Woogie was Chicago, where the leading exponents were Jimmy Yancey, the city's most popular pianist, and Clarence "Pine Top" Smith, who taught piano and wrote the legendary Pine Top's Boogie Woogie. It is quite likely that this title gave the style its famous name.

Narration

In the spring the butterflies come –
Fluttering, sparkling in the sun.
From secret hiding places, where
They spent the winter sleeping there.

SONG ONE

BUTTERFLY SPARKLE

BUTTERFLIES' DANCE

1. **Butterfly sparkle, butterfly sparkle,
Flutter by, past my window.
Such a beautiful sight,
With colours so bright.
There's red and yellow and blue and white.**

BUTTERFLIES' DANCE

2. **Butterfly sparkle, butterfly sparkle,
Pretty as petals in the sky.
You flutter together,
Light as a feather.
Please can I be a butterfly?**

BUTTERFLIES' DANCE

Narration

The butterflies so hard to catch,
Lay their eggs and then they hatch.

Look out Dad, look out Mum –
This is the time when the caterpillars come.

Yum, yum, yum and munch, munch, munch,
They're coming to your garden
For dinner, tea and lunch.

Yum, yum, yum and munch, munch, munch,
They're coming to your garden
For dinner, tea and lunch.

CATERPILLAR BOOGIE

CATERPILLARS' DANCE

Round and round the garden
On a million feet.
Caterpillars marching
To a boogie beat.
Wriggle, wriggle, wriggle, wrig-gl-ing,
On the way,
Got to find a lot of leaves
To eat today.
Green and brown and furry,
Looking out for a treat.
Lots of lovely lettuces
And cabbage to eat.

CATERPILLARS' DANCE

Round and round the garden . . .

Narration

But there are many dangers
For a little caterpillar.
Not everybody likes them,
And they make a tasty dinner!

HIP-HOP, HERE COME THE BIRDS

1. Hip-hop, hip-hop, here come the birds.
   Coming to get you caterpillars,
   Peck-peck, peck-peck, look out, they're here.
   Caterpillars, caterpillars.
   Better disappear.

2. Gardener, gardener, coming your way.
   Coming to get you caterpillars,
   With his nasty chemical spray.
   Caterpillars, caterpillars.
   Better run away.

Narration

The caterpillars eat and eat
Until they're very fat.
They'll soon turn into butterflies.
How can they do that?

They'll find a place to hide,
And then they will begin.
Round and round their bodies,
A magic web to spin.

And there are special words for this –
Pupa, cocoon and chrysalis.

SONG FOUR

CATERPILLAR LULLABY

Children gently spin threads

1. **Spin your silky silver thread.**
    Round and round it goes.
    Caterpillars disappear
    As the pupa grows.

    Children gently spin threads

2. **Sleep inside your chrysalis**
    Now that it is spun.
    Soon you'll wake as butterflies
    And sparkle in the sun.

    Spinning stops and children sleep

    SILENCE

Narration

And so the chrysalis breaks.   *(clap hands)*
And the butterfly awakes.   *(closed fists open into butterfly wings – join thumbs)*

Fly, butterfly, fly!   *(flutter hands, as a butterfly)*

20

FLY, BUTTERFLY, FLY

All children flutter their butterfly hands and the butterflies dance.

Fly, butterfly, fly,
Come on and try.
You've got to spread your new wings.   } twice
Fly, butterfly, fly
Into the big new summer blue sky.

Now you are free,
Fly where the soft winds take you.
Now you can be
Free as air the whole day through.

Fly, butterfly, fly,
Come on and try.
You've got to spread your new wings.
Fly, butterfly, fly
Into the big new summer blue sky.

Butterflies dance and come to rest during Coda

Narration   We hope you have enjoyed our show.
Just one more thing before we go.

A big long word for your big word list –
If you want to study butterflies you'll be a
LEPIDOPTERIST!

Everyone   Bye-bye.

Wave and exit to a repeat of song two **CATERPILLAR BOOGIE**

THE END

1
BUTTERFLY SPARKLE

Cue: They spent the winter sleeping there.

Both hand play an octave up throughout
Ped. ad lib throughout

Butterflies' Dance

(melody is played over a C chord)

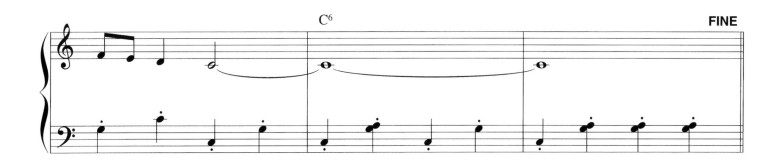

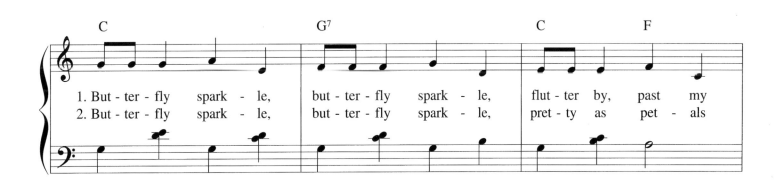

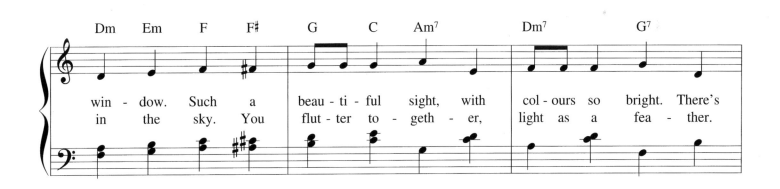

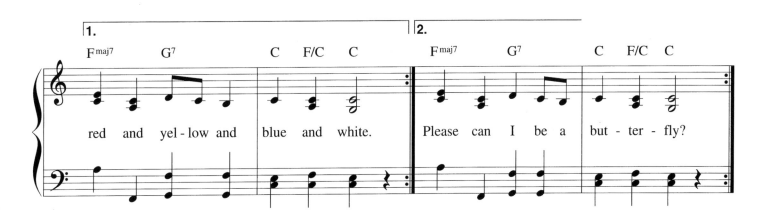

2
CATERPILLAR BOOGIE (also music for finale)

Cue: They're coming to your garden for dinner, tea and lunch.

Caterpillars' Dance

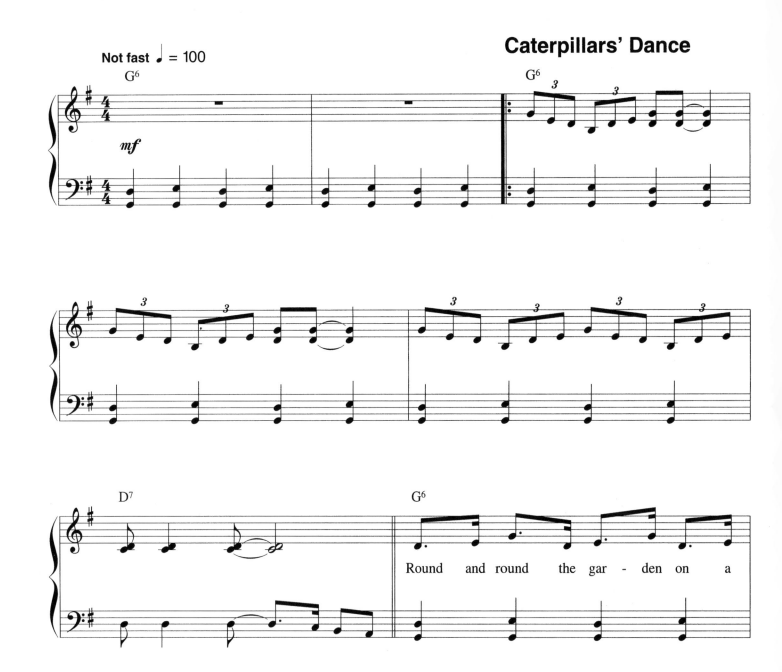

Round and round the gar - den on a

mil - li - on feet.___ Cat - er - pil - lars march - ing to a

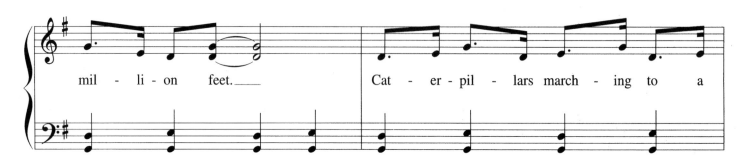

See page 17 for What Is A Boogie?

3
HIP-HOP, HERE COME THE BIRDS

Cue: Not everybody likes them, and they make a tasty dinner!

Lyrics under the music:

1. Hip - hop, hip - hop, here come the birds. Com - ing to get you cat - er - pil - lars,
2. Gar - dener, gar - dener, com - ing your way.

peck - peck, peck - peck, look out, they're here. Cat - er - pil - lars, cat - er - pil - lars.
with his nas - ty chem - i - cal spray.

Bet - ter dis - ap - pear.
Bet - ter run a - way.

4
CATERPILLAR LULLABY

Cue: Pupa, cocoon and chrysalis.

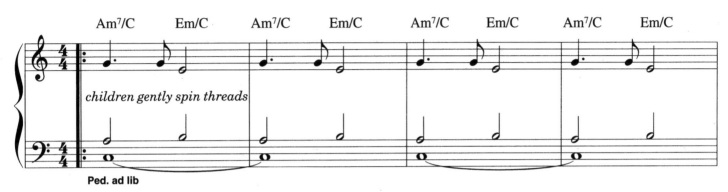

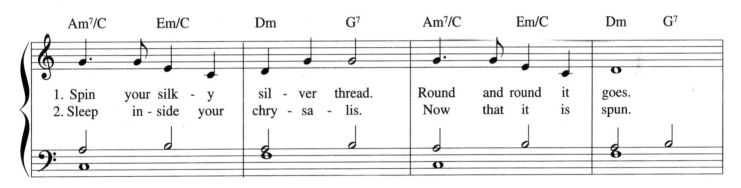

Spin your silk-y sil-ver thread. Round and round it goes.
Sleep in-side your chry-sa-lis. Now that it is spun.

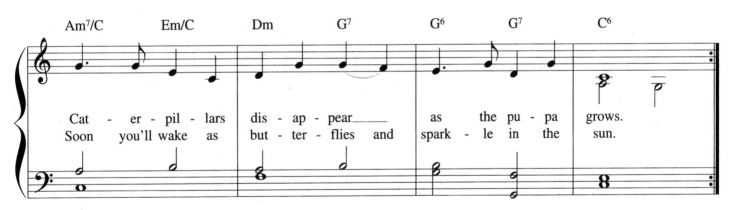

Cat-er-pil-lars dis-ap-pear___ as the pu-pa grows.
Soon you'll wake as but-ter-flies and spark-le in the sun.

Coda

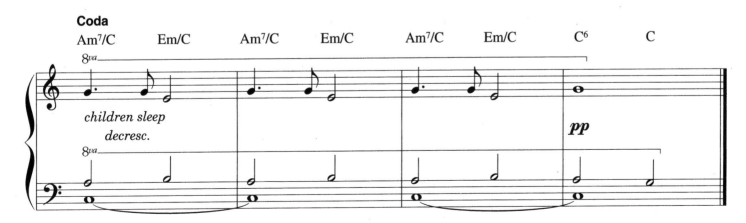

5
FLY, BUTTERFLY, FLY

Cue: Fly, butterfly, fly! (flutter hands as a butterfly)

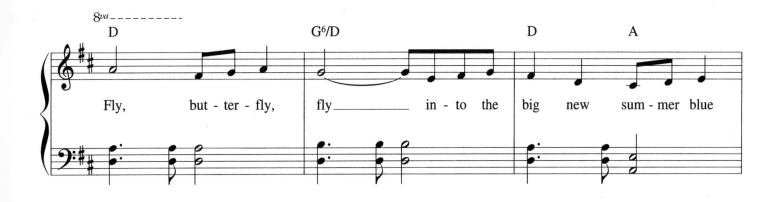

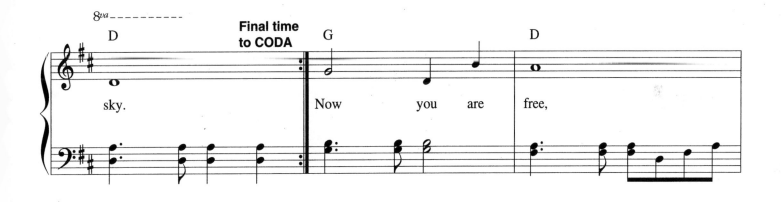

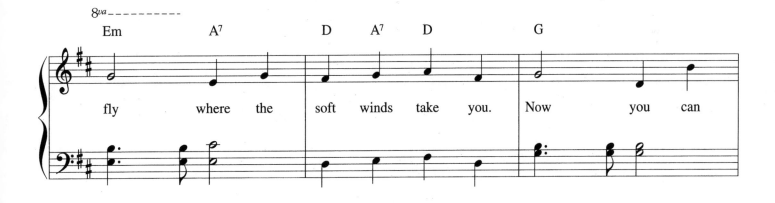

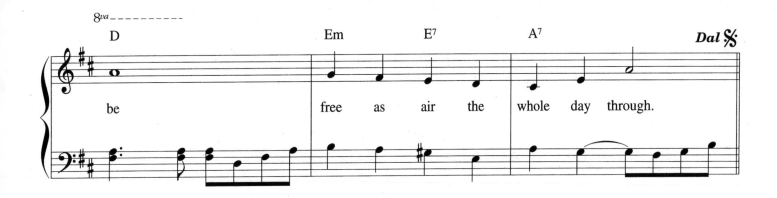

CODA

Repeat Song 2 CATERPILLAR BOOGIE (page 24) for children to wave and exit (finale)

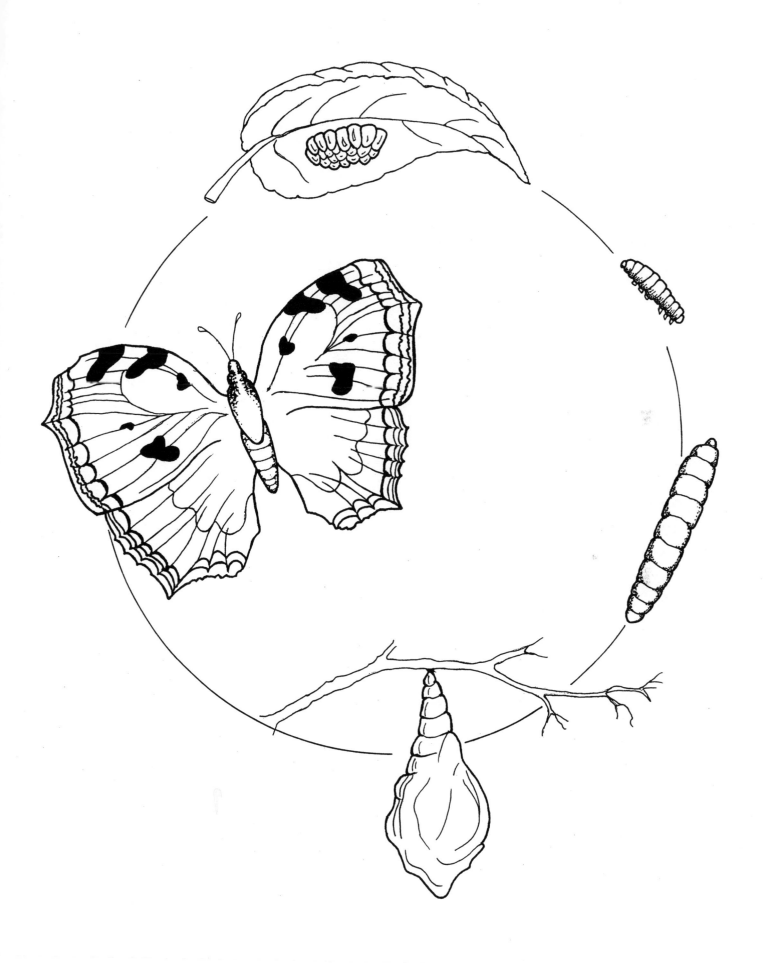

CD TRACK LISTING

Full performances...

TADPOLE RAG
1. Song 1 – Frog Song
2. Song 2 – Something Squidgy
3. Song 3 – Tadpole Rag
4. Song 4 – Quack!
5. Song 5 – Frogs Are Amazing
6. Repeat Song 3 – Tadpole Rag

CATERPILLAR BOOGIE
7. Song 1 – Butterfly Sparkle
8. Song 2 – Caterpillar Boogie
9. Song 3 – Hip-Hop, Here Come The Birds
10. Song 4 – Caterpillar Lullaby
11. Song 5 – Fly, Butterfly, Fly
12. Repeat Song 2 – Caterpillar Boogie

Backing tracks only...

TADPOLE RAG
13. Song 1 – Frog Song
14. Song 2 – Something Squidgy
15. Song 3 – Tadpole Rag
16. Song 4 – Quack!
17. Song 5 – Frogs Are Amazing
18. Repeat Song 3 – Tadpole Rag

CATERPILLAR BOOGIE
19. Song 1 – Butterfly Sparkle
20. Song 2 – Caterpillar Boogie
21. Song 3 – Hip-Hop, Here Come The Birds
22. Song 4 – Caterpillar Lullaby
23. Song 5 – Fly, Butterfly, Fly
24. Repeat Song 2 – Caterpillar Boogie

To remove your CD from the plastic sleeve, lift the small lip on the side to break the perforated flap. Replace the disc after use for convenient storage.